The Great Benin Empire

+234express®

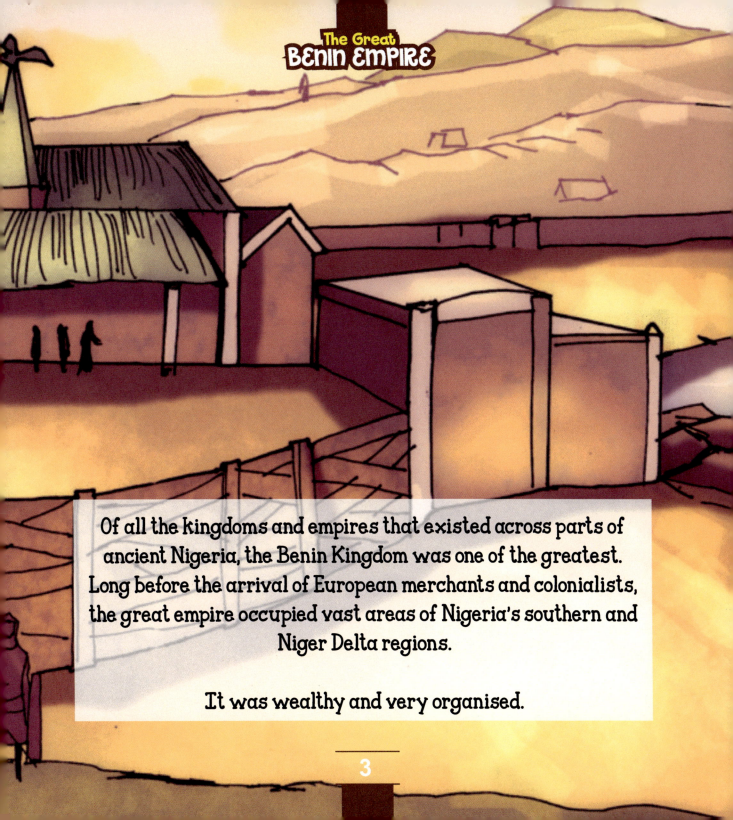

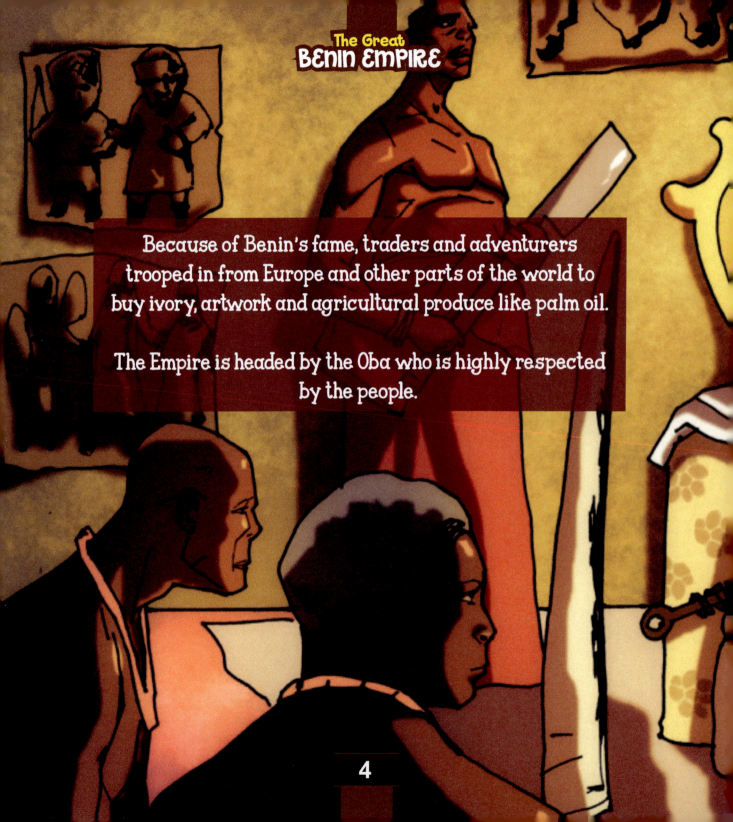

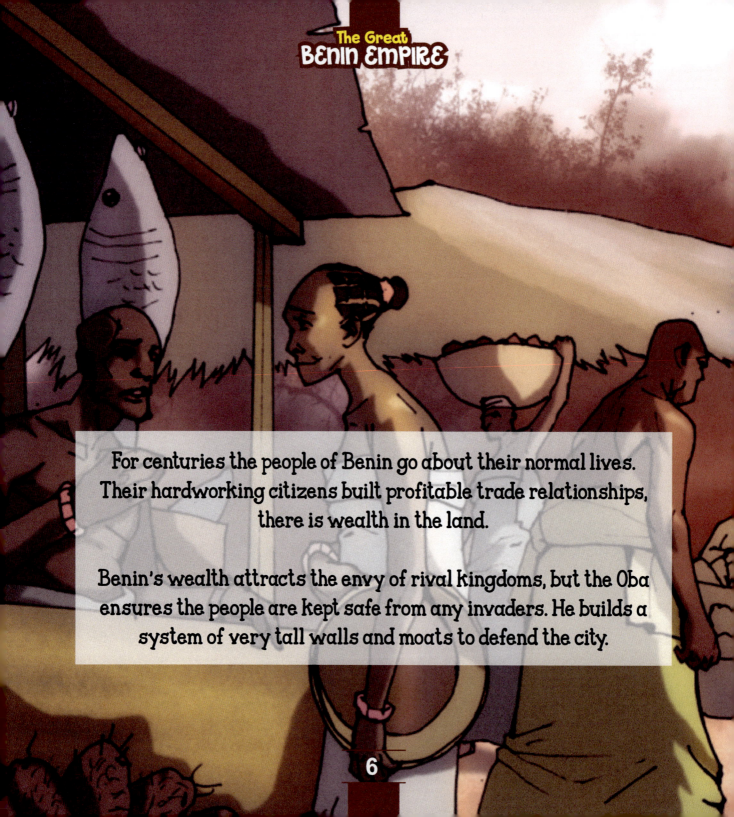

The Great Benin Empire

For centuries the people of Benin go about their normal lives. Their hardworking citizens built profitable trade relationships, there is wealth in the land.

Benin's wealth attracts the envy of rival kingdoms, but the Oba ensures the people are kept safe from any invaders. He builds a system of very tall walls and moats to defend the city.

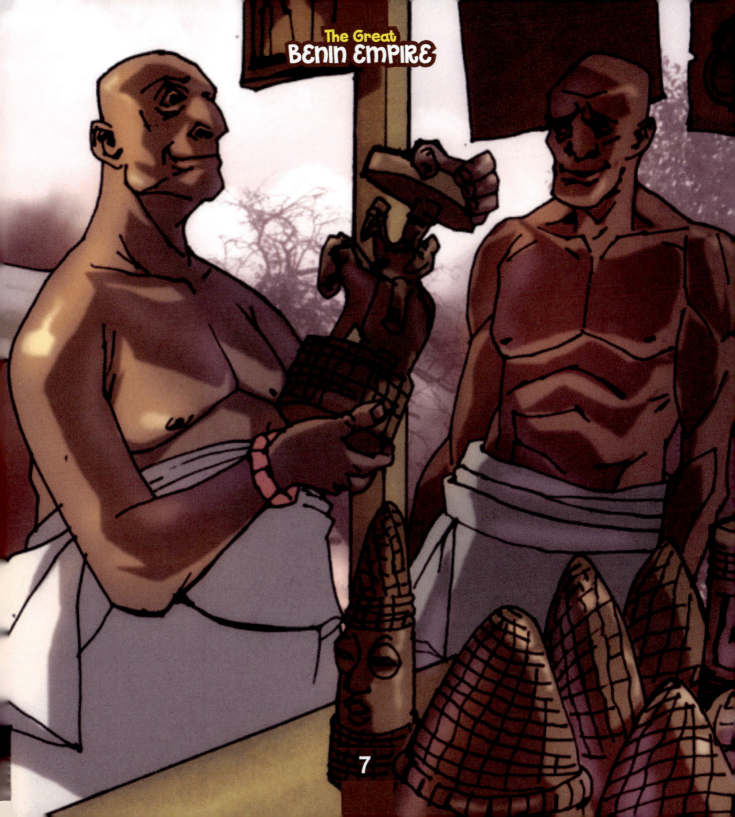

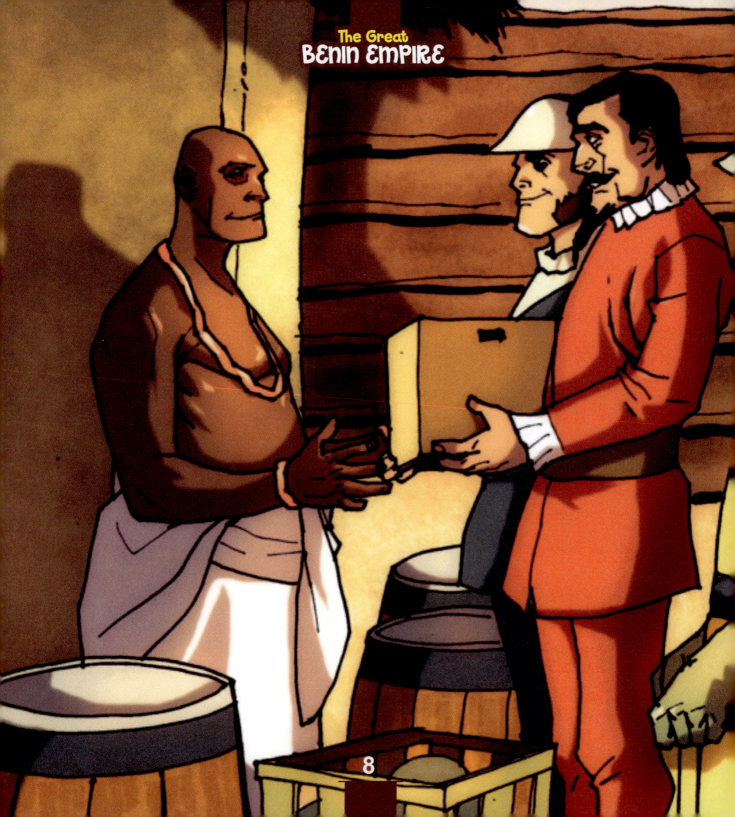

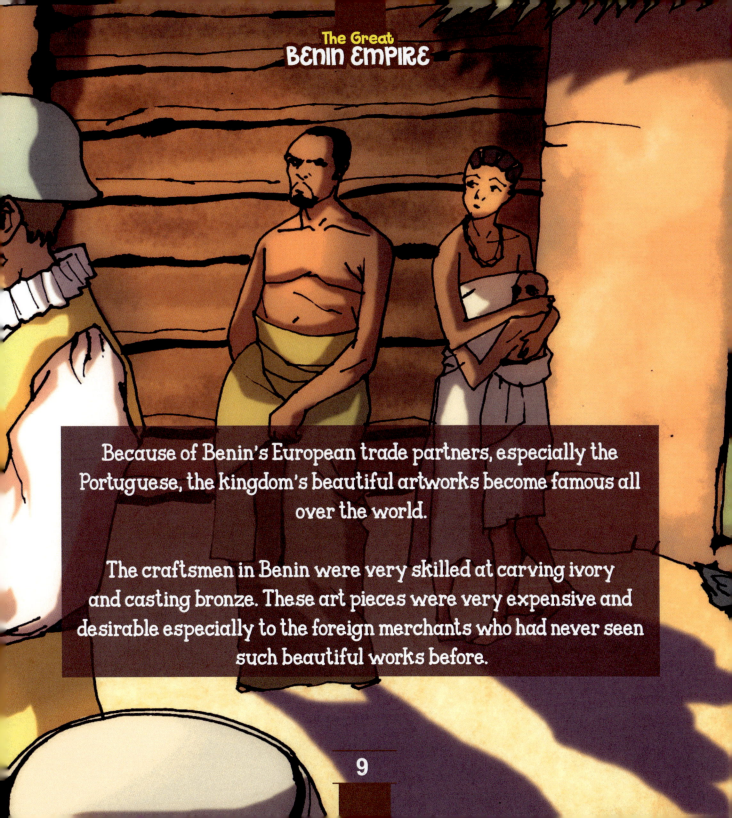

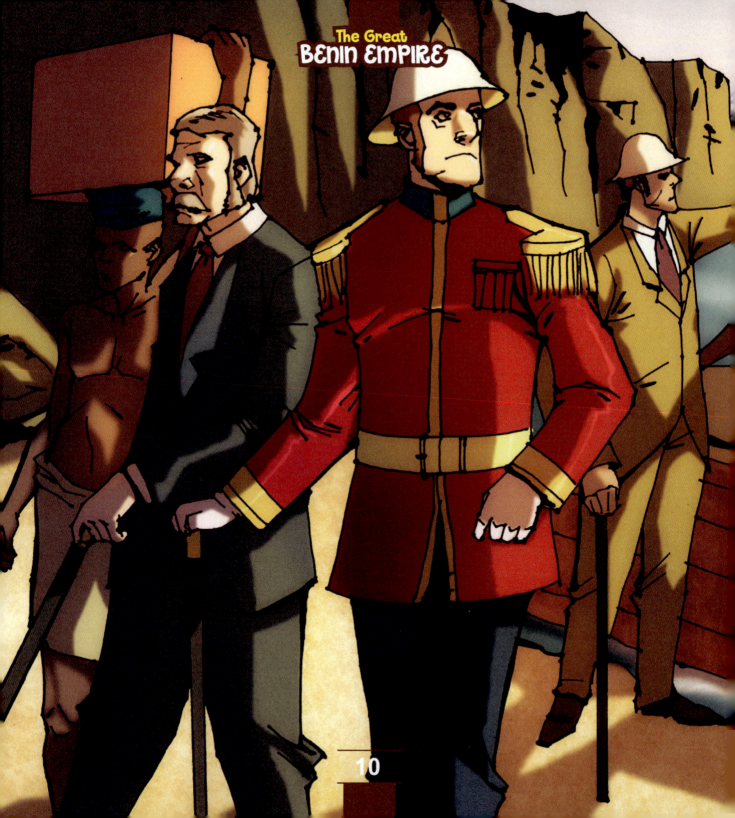

At Benin, Oba Ovonramen knew that the British wanted to take over his land. He knew they had deceived or forced the people of Lagos and other parts of the Niger Delta to give up their sovereignty.

When a group of British colonialists and officers visit him at his palace in 1890, he refused to sign any trade or protection deals with them.

The Great Benin Empire

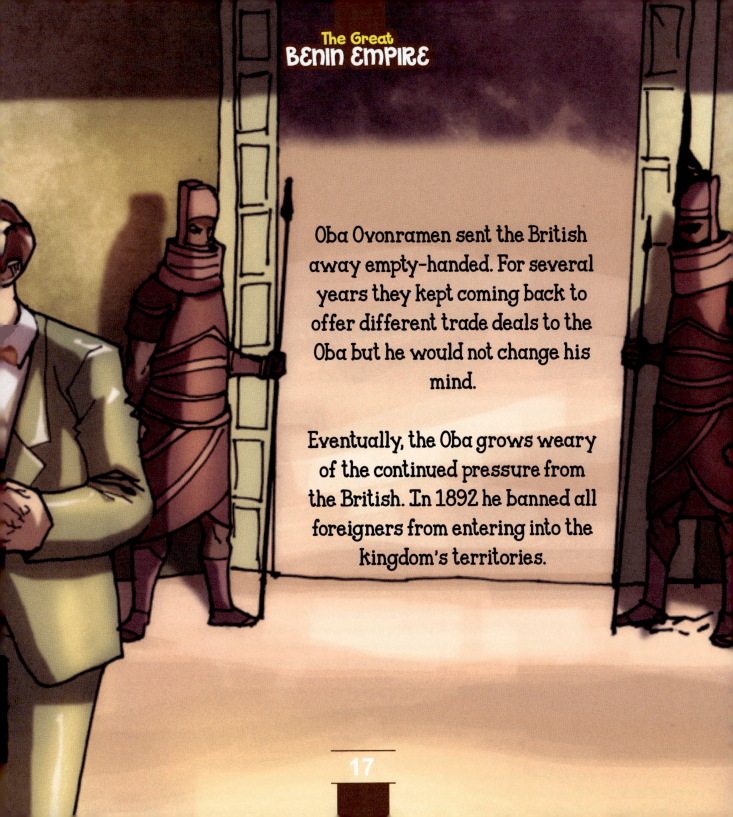

Oba Ovonramen sent the British away empty-handed. For several years they kept coming back to offer different trade deals to the Oba but he would not change his mind.

Eventually, the Oba grows weary of the continued pressure from the British. In 1892 he banned all foreigners from entering into the kingdom's territories.

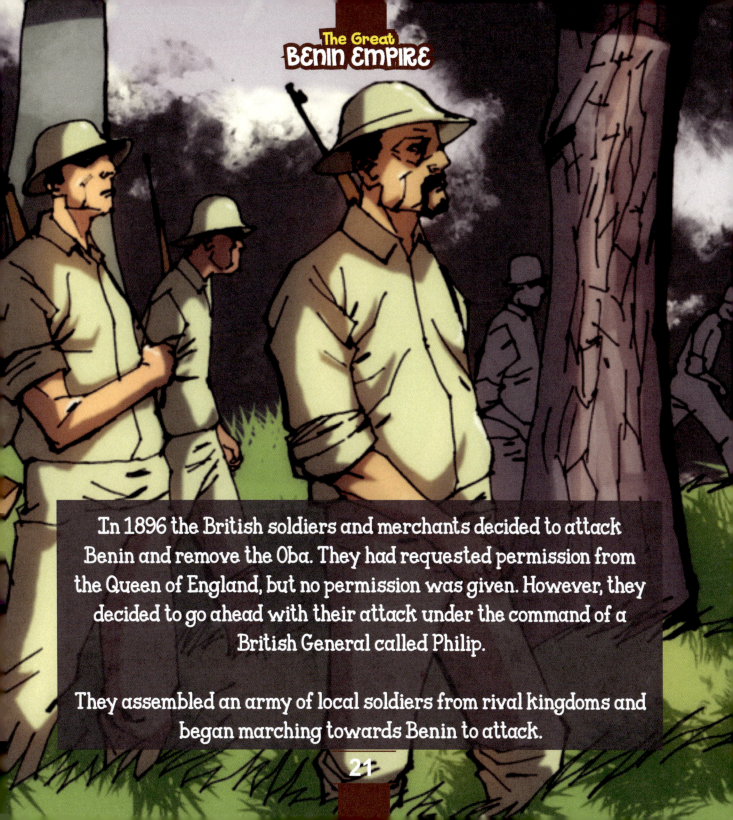

In 1896 the British soldiers and merchants decided to attack Benin and remove the Oba. They had requested permission from the Queen of England, but no permission was given. However, they decided to go ahead with their attack under the command of a British General called Philip.

They assembled an army of local soldiers from rival kingdoms and began marching towards Benin to attack.

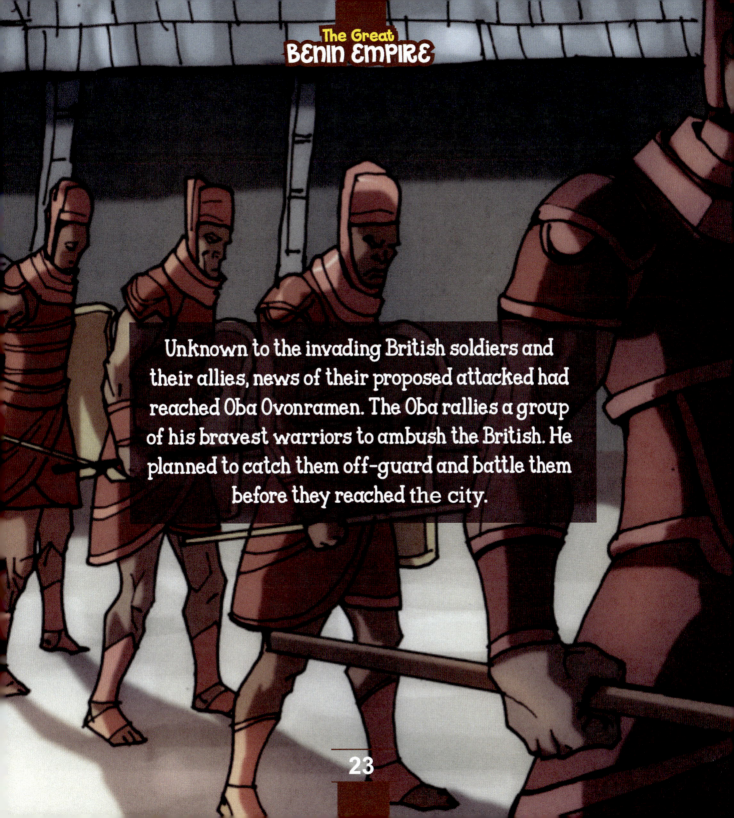

The Great Benin Empire

Unknown to the invading British soldiers and their allies, news of their proposed attacked had reached Oba Ovonramen. The Oba rallies a group of his bravest warriors to ambush the British. He planned to catch them off-guard and battle them before they reached the city.

The Great Benin Empire

General Philip's men had camped a few miles from Benin in a place called Gwato to prepare for the attack on the city. The ambush planned by the Oba's warriors catch the British contingent completely off-guard and the invaders are defeated.

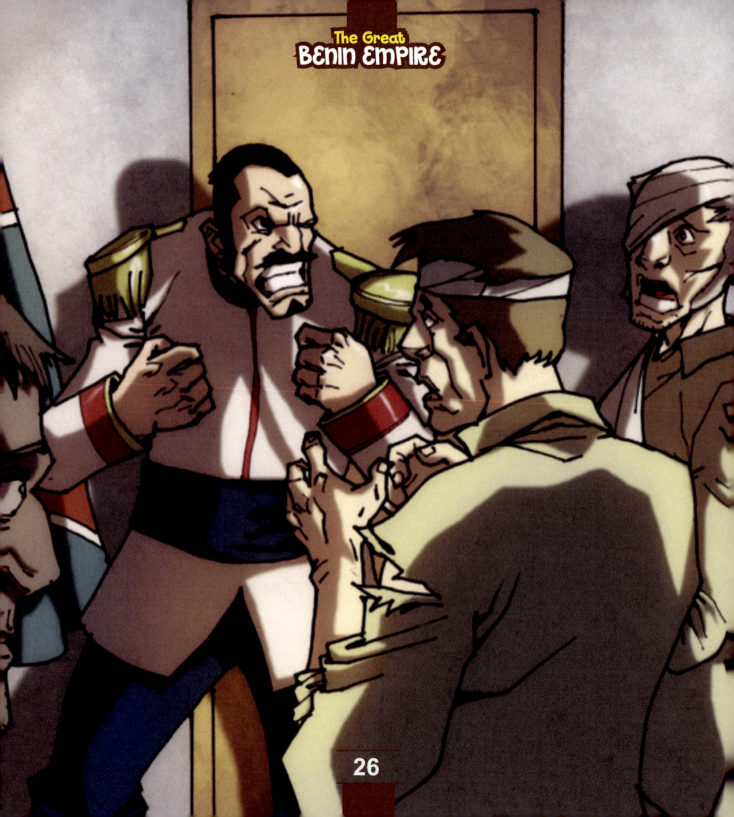

The Great BENIN EMPIRE

Some of the British soldiers and their allies escaped from the battle at Gwato and retreated to Lagos.

They had underestimated the Oba's will to protect his kingdom and people. They paid dearly for their greed and arrogance.

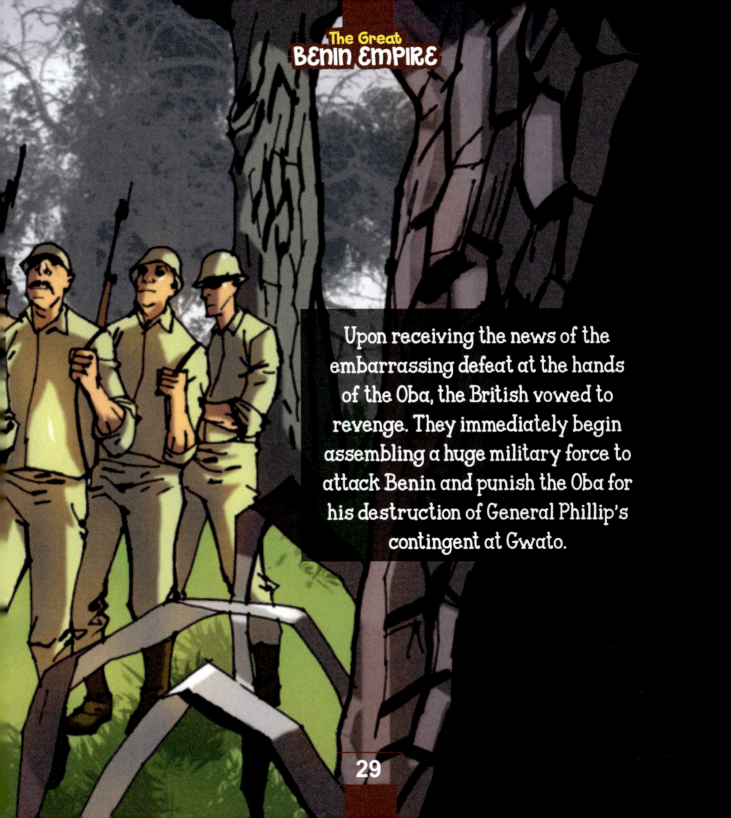

The Great BENIN EMPIRE

Upon receiving the news of the embarrassing defeat at the hands of the Oba, the British vowed to revenge. They immediately begin assembling a huge military force to attack Benin and punish the Oba for his destruction of General Phillip's contingent at Gwato.

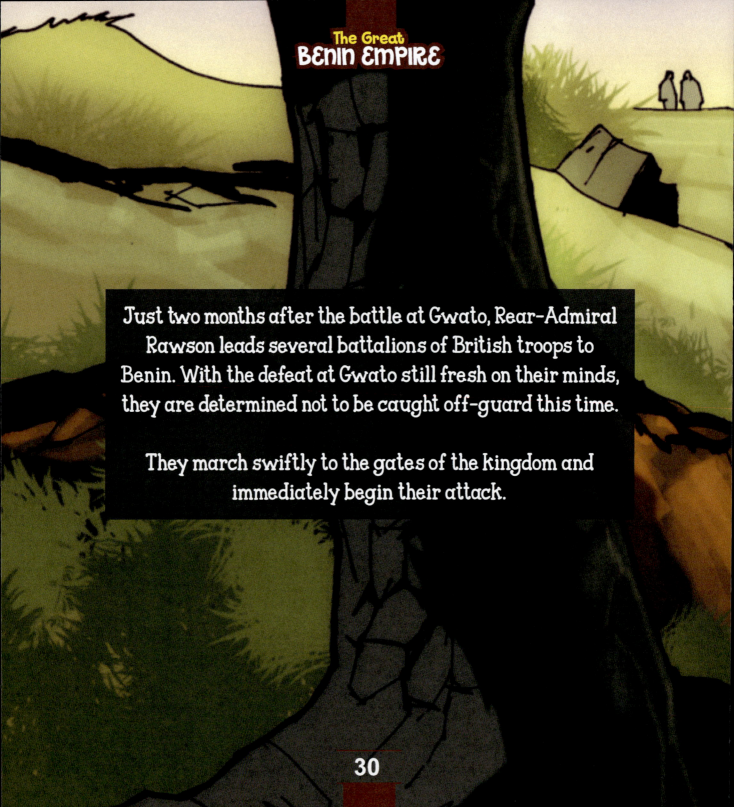

The Great BENIN EMPIRE

Just two months after the battle at Gwato, Rear-Admiral Rawson leads several battalions of British troops to Benin. With the defeat at Gwato still fresh on their minds, they are determined not to be caught off-guard this time.

They march swiftly to the gates of the kingdom and immediately begin their attack.

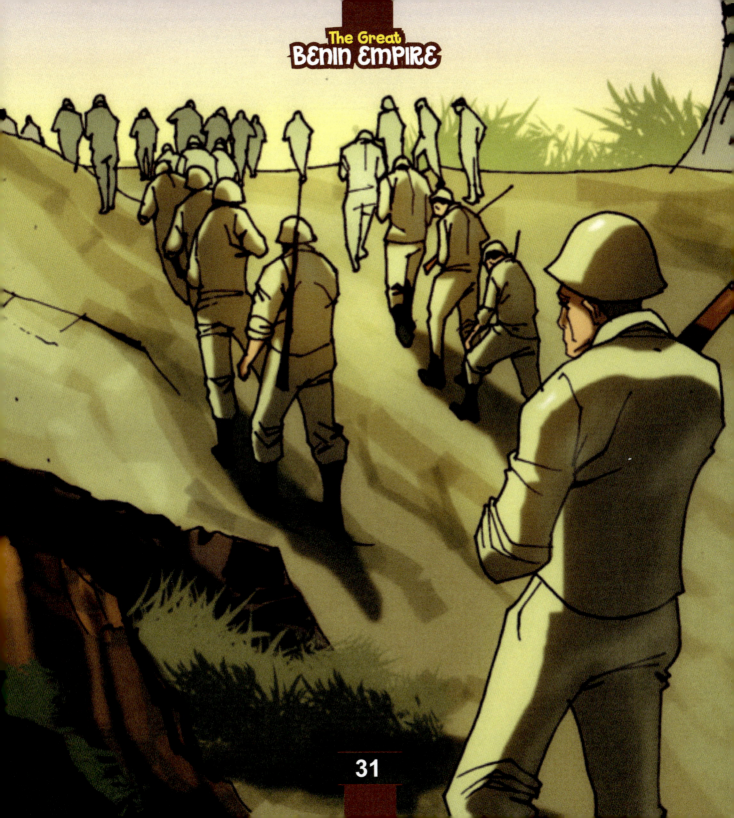

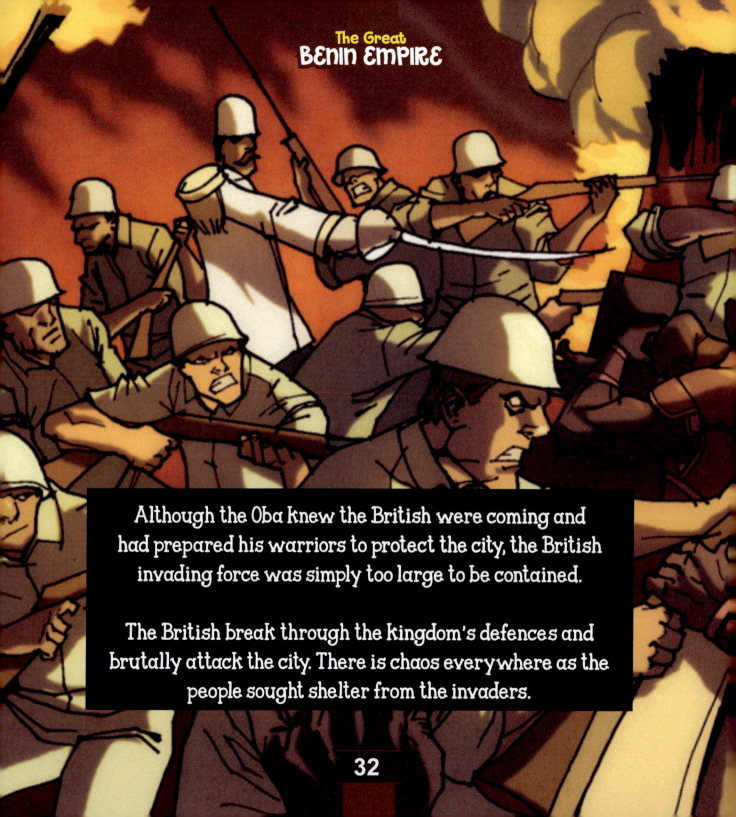

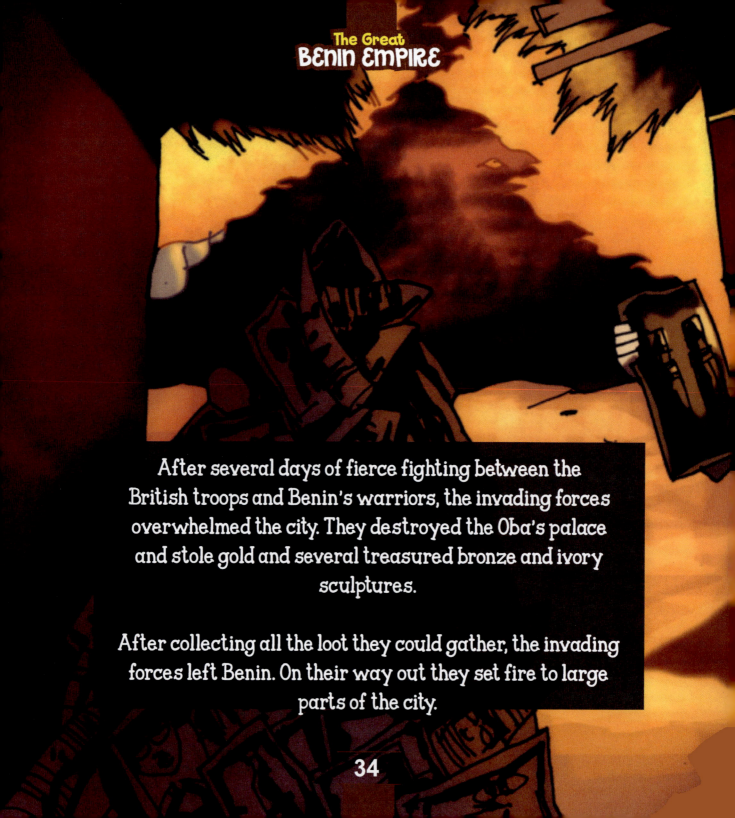

The Great BENIN EMPIRE

After several days of fierce fighting between the British troops and Benin's warriors, the invading forces overwhelmed the city. They destroyed the Oba's palace and stole gold and several treasured bronze and ivory sculptures.

After collecting all the loot they could gather, the invading forces left Benin. On their way out they set fire to large parts of the city.

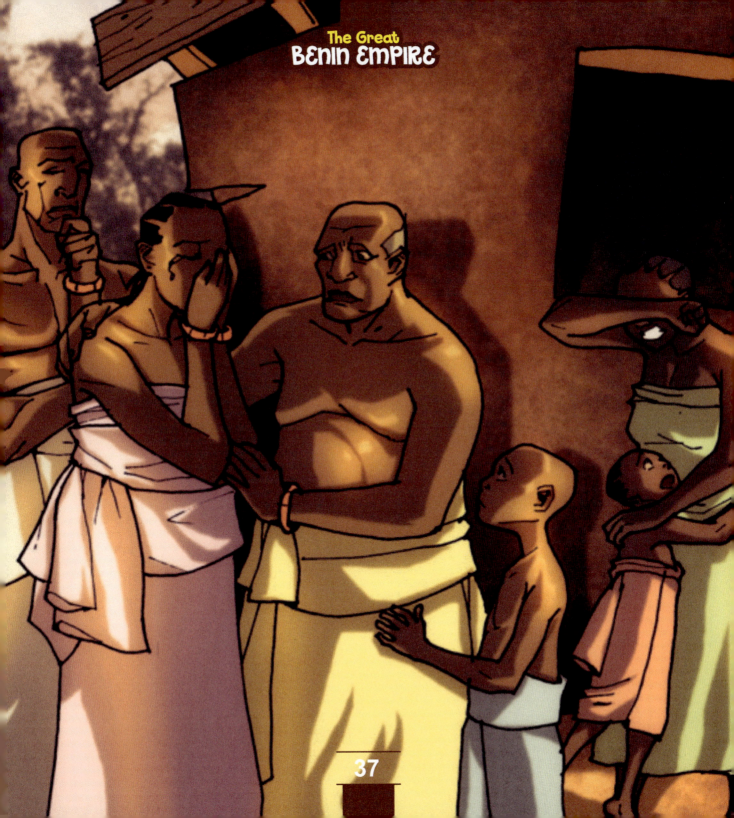

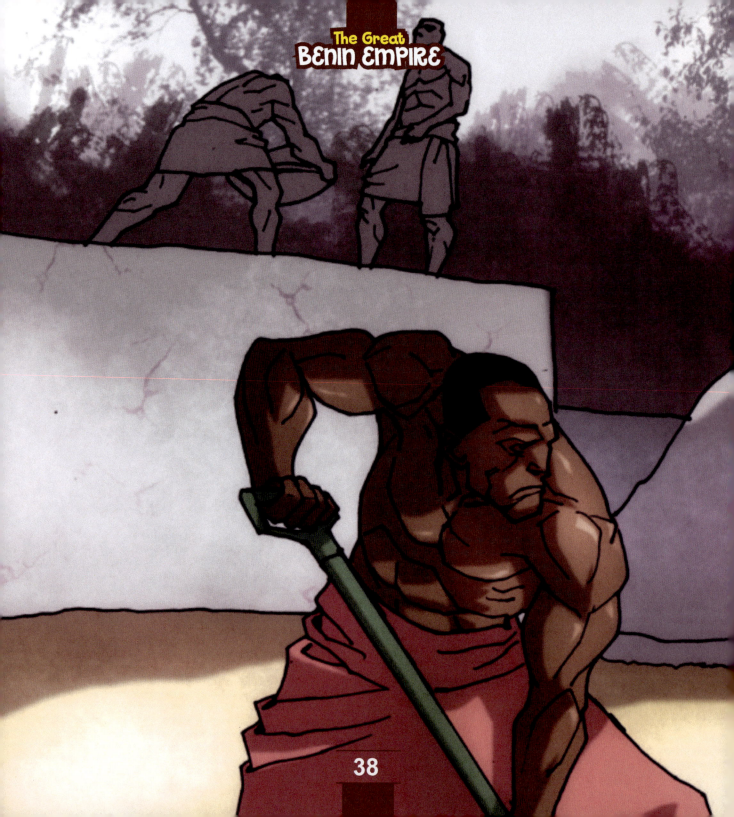

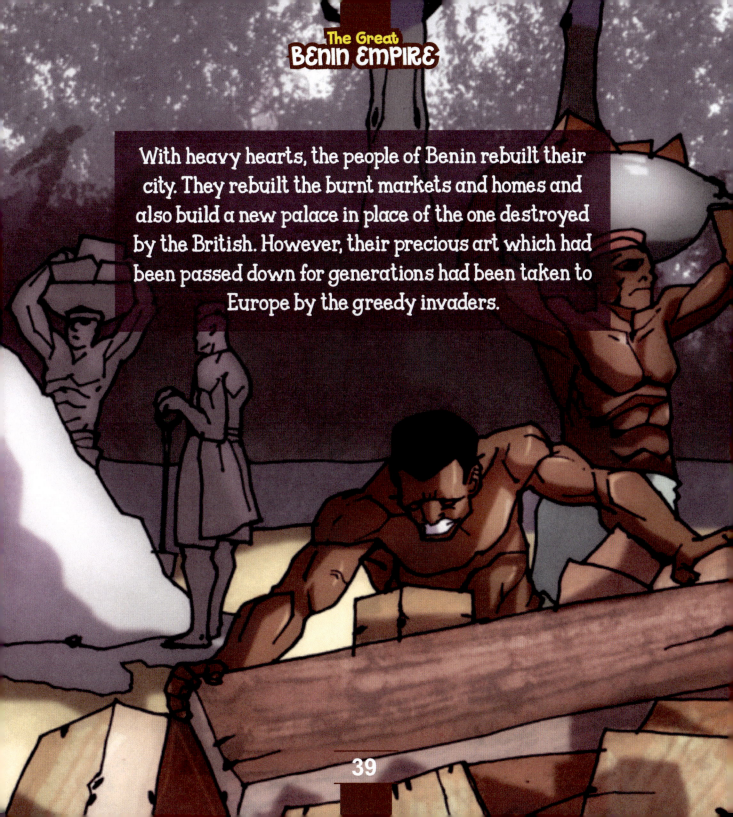

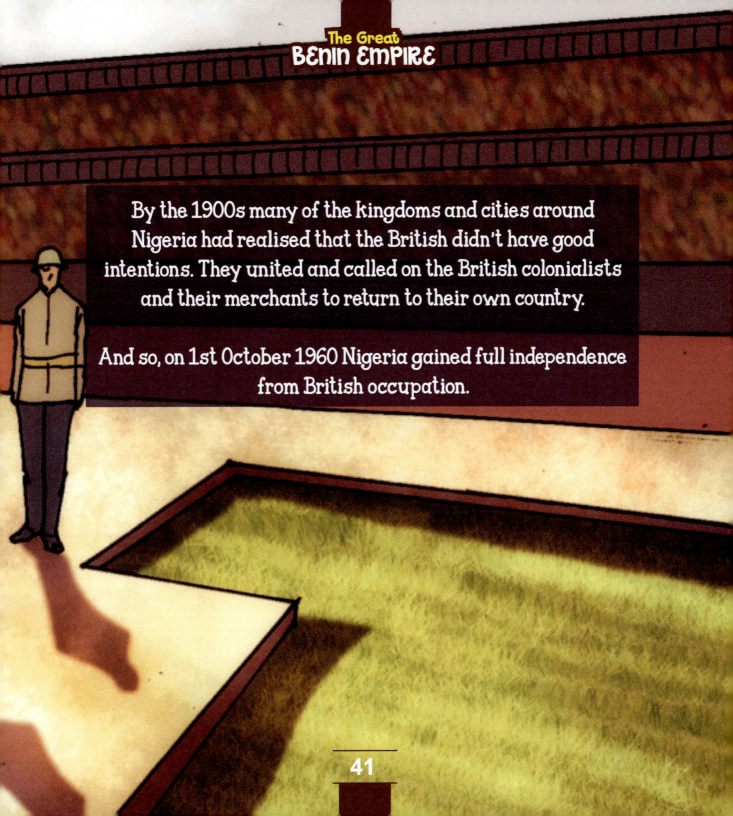

The Great BENIN EMPIRE

By the 1900s many of the kingdoms and cities around Nigeria had realised that the British didn't have good intentions. They united and called on the British colonialists and their merchants to return to their own country.

And so, on 1st October 1960 Nigeria gained full independence from British occupation.

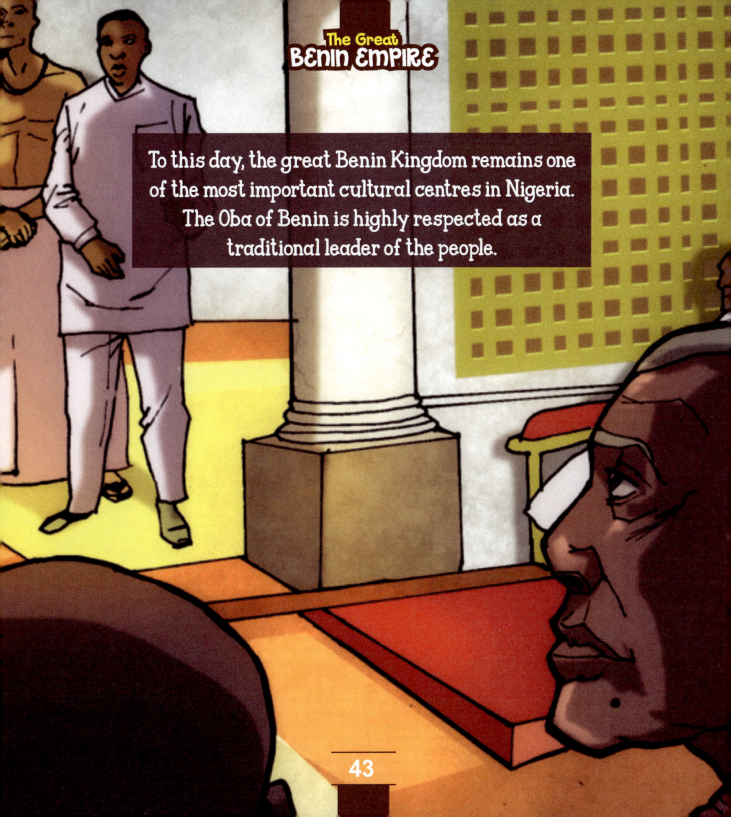

Manufactured by Amazon.ca
Bolton, ON